To Jane

May Love, Light, and Peace
be with you always.

Douglas Taylor

The most incomprehensible thing about the universe is that it is comprehensible.
—Albert Einstein

THE LIGHTHOUSE

If in our journey, we lose our way
Remember always we must not stay
Lost in the past of yesterday
Our true home beckons, with guiding light
We must follow bravely from inner sight
The future's brilliance seen as we roam
Will always guide us back to our home

Soulic Journeys

A Visionary Guide to Spiritual Enlightenment
Douglas Taylor

FLIGHT OF THE PHOENIX

Crystalvision Creations

ISBN 0-9704593-0-0

©2000 Douglas Taylor

Printed in Korea

Published by Crystalvision Creations

1846 Main Street, Huntington Beach, CA 92648

E-mail: dougt@surfside.net

Dedication

I would like to humbly thank the many great minds that, through borrowed quotations, have contributed their timeless wisdom to this book. Without their strength and courage to forge ahead in the face of constant opposition, our civilization would be a barren and primitive land. I hope this book can serve as an example of my own life-changing healing experiences attained through expressing art and creativity, in this way helping others to discover that inspiration flows endlessly to all those who can feel its subtle message of love, joy, and serenity, in all acts of creative expression.

Contents

Paintings

Acknowledgements

I would like to thank the following people for their loving contributions to this book. To Lianne and Joseph Downey for their masterful editing of the text. Tony Glinkas who was always there to lend a helping hand and designed the cover and the back of the book. Michael Leas for his creative printing expertise in helping to get this project off the ground. And to Alan McGowan for his eagle eye in correcting the text. Last but not least, to Uriel, without whose help this book would never have been possible.

STAIRWAY TO THE STARS

The Beginning of Our Journey

How can we rise above the limitations that seemingly surround us, imprisoning our thoughts in mundane repetitious patterns? What is life's great secret that gives gifts of such unique creative abilities to certain people? And does everyone have a natural relationship to Universal forces from which we can draw a never-ending supply of inspiration?

These questions can form the springboard from which we can project our minds into a unique visionary world, a powerful creative realm of limitless possibilities that can expand and enlighten our perception of reality. As we open our minds to a brave new world through these simple questions, we can now relax, sit back and enjoy the adventure.

I don't know what I may seem to the world, but as to myself, I seem to have been only like a boy playing on the seashore and diverting myself in now and then finding a smoother pebble or a prettier shell than ordinary, whilst the great ocean of truth lay all undiscovered before me.

—Sir Isaac Newton

Introduction

Twenty-five years ago, if someone had told me that I would be writing a book someday, I would have thought they were crazy! What would I possibly write about? The only thing I knew how to do or even wanted to do was surf—following the endless summer around the world searching for the perfect wave—and this is exactly what I did. I wasn't interested in family life, and relationships with women always left me feeling like I was making a mistake, and that I had better not get involved in something that might interfere with my surfing schedule.

Neither would I have believed that I would become an artist, as I never had any interest in that area. Yet now at the age of forty-four, creative expression has become the most enjoyable and spiritually stimulating activity in my life! My life has become a great adventure, with inspiration flowing through my mind in powerful bursts of rainbow-hued colors, taking me on a wondrous journey far beyond my previous limitations and beliefs.

How did these seemingly miraculous changes come into my life? That is the story I wish to share with you, as I feel truly fortunate to have the opportunity to write and paint and experience all this creative enthusiasm.

I have learned that creative expression is a direct line to the Universal forces that can and will inspire us in every aspect of our lives. True inspiration comes as an uplifting power, helping us to overcome our limitations. It is never meant for selfish purposes but to inspire others to develop to their highest potential. In my art I attempt to carry this message of inspiration. Excellence in any field is a product of a synthesis of the mind, body, and spirit. The messenger is unimportant and transitory, but the message is eternal.

The ability to paint, write, play music, or express yourself in any inspired or creative endeavor has long been considered a gift given to special people favored by God or some Universal power. Men and women such as Leonardo da Vinci, Joan of Arc, Michelangelo, Wolfgang Amadeus Mozart, Marie Curie, Nikola Tesla, Albert Einstein, etc., have positively transformed our world through the power of their creative and inspired expressions. What unique characteristics allowed these creative thinkers to express their talents in such advanced and superior ways? And how can we as common mortals ever rise above the mundane limitations that seem to strangle and block our own creative potential? Research into the lives of these creative geniuses would benefit our search for these answers, yet it still would not reveal the source of their inspiration.

Science and art have been recognized by great thinkers, such as Leonardo da Vinci, to have parallels on a much deeper level than meets the eye. The nature of perception and the physical laws that are expressed uniformly throughout the universe were recognized by Leonardo and utilized in the creation of his many artistic masterpieces. His creative mind was ever at work with designs and inventions that were far ahead of his time. Joan of Arc suffered a martyr's death, being burned at the stake at the tender age of nineteen for her incredible feat of inspiring an entire country to rise above the tyranny of their English oppressors. She has since been canonized and is still inspiring people worldwide with her amazing example of spiritual strength and courage.

Albert Einstein, one of the greatest scientific minds of modern times, was once quoted as saying, "Imagination is more important than knowledge." Imagination, according to *Webster's* definition, is "the act or power of forming mental images of what is not present, or the act or power of creating new ideas by combining previous experiences." Intuition and imagination have been utilized by all the great creative minds of the past.

Intuition, taken from the Latin word *intueri,* which means to look at from within, begins a definition of inspiration. We can take this a little further and define inspiration as the ability to sense intuitive guidance and the inner strength to follow this direction, regardless of established rules, regulations, or conformities within society. This willingness to break away from the commonly accepted parameters of thought and action was demonstrated in the unique creative genius of both Michelangelo and Nikola Tesla.

Tesla, the inventor of alternating current generators and a long list of inspired devices and futuristic designs, often related how he could see his inventions completed mentally, and he would build the working model without any experimentation! His ability to tune into this universal, creative source freed his mind to express its true creative nature.

This mental process is purely scientific, similar to the radio or television where the receiver dials a specific station and then, through frequency compatibility, the mind receives the information from the transmitter. The transmitter exists in another realm or dimension which can be called God or Infinite Creative Intelligence. The quality of the information is totally dependent on the ability of the receiver to align mentally with the creative flow of his or her inner spiritual self. Selfish or self-centered motivation will always weaken the connection and can eventually short-circuit this electronic process.

Michelangelo once said of his sculptures that the masterpiece already existed within the stone and all he did was release it from its rocky prison.

Marie Curie, the first woman to win the Nobel Prize, was a brilliant and respected physicist, challenging the male-dominated society to begin to recognize women as peers and, in some cases superior to their male contemporaries. She was also the first person to win this most prestigious award, the Nobel Prize, twice.

Wolfgang Amadeus Mozart was writing and playing inspired music at the age of five. What can explain such precocious genius proclivities?

In this book, we will explore this unique phenomenon, this science of inspiration, and answer such questions as where does inspiration come from? And, as in the case of Mozart, how can someone express such phenomenal talents at such a young age?

But even more than this, we will embark upon an adventure, a visionary journey if you will, into a futuristic realm where intuition, imagination, and inspiration blend together to form realities far beyond our accepted limitations. A place where light, color, and form harmonize with nature, in all its magnificent beauty—thus awakening us to the Spiritual reality of life as it unfolds, similar to the flower, in countless patterns, forever growing toward that great Spiritual Sun of Infinity.

Those who live in the attractive force of love achieve harmony with nature and their fellow beings.

—Paramahansa Yogananda

MYSTIC ISLES

Nature, The Environment, and Art

Human history becomes more and more a race between education and catastrophe.
—H.G. Wells

Nature has no doubt been the greatest source of inspiration for artists throughout history, and it has had a powerful rejuvenation in our present day. As we collectively begin to realize the importance of conservation and protection of wildlife habitats, a pitched battle has ensued between environmentalists and industrialization. The future of a skyrocketing global population and worldwide environmental pollution has inspired many people to take action in circumventing the very real danger of environmental genocide. Artists have the unique opportunity to depict the great importance and value of nature through art, without the need of preaching, as realistic portrayals of the natural world speak for themselves.

NATURE'S CALLING

A thing of beauty is a joy forever. Its loveliness increases; it will never pass into nothingness.

—John Keats

The magnificent Bald Eagles, masters of the sky, and the streamlined, powerful Orcas, masters of the sea, are certainly worthy of our respect, admiration, and most of all our protection. They are no doubt some of nature's most beautiful artistic creations.

EAGLES AND ORCAS

PACIFIC NORTHWEST MOONRISE

6

How inappropriate to call this planet Earth
when clearly it is Ocean.

—Arthur C. Clark

OCEAN'S SONG
Oh beautiful Ocean, Oh powerful sea
I must surrender myself to thee
Your crystalline waves enrapture my mind
With sparkling treasures in which I find
Such peace and joy of a watery kind

GOLDENWEST SUNSET

Surfing and riding waves, while being exhilarating, has always given me a sense of appreciation of nature and its ceaseless wonders. Riding on the crest of a large wave could be compared to a mixture of ballet and bullfighting, with a rainbow-colored background of awe-inspiring beauty.

It's with my brush I make love.
—Pierre Auguste Renoir

SURF CITY

The shape of a great wave, like the shape of a beautiful woman, can excite a myriad of emotions, from anticipatory desire to ecstasy followed by satisfaction. Two of nature's marvelous creations which continue to inspire artists and surfers alike.

A man travels the world in search of what he needs and returns home to find it.
　　　　　　　　—George Moore

PARADISE FOUND

For many years of my youth I thought paradise could be found in some location, with perfect waves breaking endlessly as the warm tropical breeze blows the fragrant scent of colorful flowers in a dreamy mixture of peace and contentment. After many years of searching I finally realized that for me, peace of mind was a very elusive condition and one that could only be found in learning to develop a stronger relationship with my inner spiritual self.

TROPICAL SPLENDOR

The artist is in his work as God is in creation, invisible and all powerful; one must sense him everywhere but never see him.

—Gustave Flaubert

It is believed that in the turbulent beginnings of our planet, the moon was much closer to us than it is today. In fact, scientists have calculated the moon's orbit receding from Earth on a yearly basis. In the four-and-a-half billion years since the estimated beginning of our solar system, the moon has taken up a much less prominent position in the sky. Surely the awesome primal forces that created our planet were following the same basic principles by which all creativity is made manifest, including art!

PRIMAL FORCES

WHALE SONG

Whales and Dolphins:
Our Water Brothers

God, or in other words, nature.

—Baruch Spinoza

Whales and Dolphins have been a favorite subject for marine artists, as they seem to exude a sense of joy and peacefulness that inspire observers to sense the innate spiritual essence that pervades all life. Many people, when experiencing close encounters with whales and dolphins, have related that it was a powerful religious or spiritual upliftment that will remain with them for a lifetime. These experiences suggest a momentary attunement with the unity and oneness with all life, which translates into a deep appreciation of our own unique place in the universe; and to hopefully recognize the great importance in seeing ourselves as caretakers of our planet and its many wonderful inhabitants.

Environmentalists make terrible neighbors but great ancestors.

— David R. Browner
Former Sierra Club Director

Dolphins throughout history have been known to be friendly characters and on numerous occasions have been responsible for saving shipwrecked seafarers from being swallowed up in Neptune's graveyard.

Countless times when out surfing, I have had the pleasure of observing these water brothers at close range and have marveled at their seeming happy-go-lucky attitude. Surfers generally consider themselves the rulers of the waves and there is a very definite pecking order based on size and experience, yet on the rare occasions when the dolphins decide to ride the waves, everyone gets out of the way and watches the true masters perform.

DOLPHINS' PLAYGROUND

The pursuit of perfection, then, is the pursuit of sweetness and light . . . He who works for sweetness and light united, works to make reason and the will of God prevail.
—Mathew Arnold

ORCHID'S ATTRACTION

The Unified Circle of Life

For those who are awake the Cosmos is one.
—Heraclitus

The unity and oneness that permeates all life can be easily recognized when our minds are absorbed in appreciating nature, even though our observations are being heavily influenced by previous ideas and beliefs based on past experiences. Yet nature has a transcendent quality, that pure essence of life that helps to free our minds and open our hearts to the awesome beauty that has always surrounded us, although often going unnoticed and unappreciated. Is it possible that the ceaseless rhythmic beat of the waves upon the shore shapes the coastline in a similar manner as our harmonious thoughts and inspirations shape the future of our civilizations? If so, then let us rejoice in our unity and dream of our positive future aspirations.

THE PULSE OF CREATION

14

The nature of God is a circle of which the center is everywhere and the circumference is nowhere.

—Empedocles

RAINBOW'S END

If I have seen further it is by standing on the shoulders of giants.

—Sir Isaac Newton

The two-way perspective has been very popular with marine artists and it is an excellent way of getting up-close-and-personal with the almost unbelievable, brilliantly-colored tropical fish and their coral reef habitats, while at the same time allowing the artist to depict the more standard seascape.

In this painting I took this technique one step further. You have the familiar underwater and above view of a beautiful tropical sunset, and also the perspective from fifty thousand miles out, and then the final view of the Milky Way galaxy itself. Our tiny blue planet is an insignificant speck in a small solar system on the inner rim of one of the Milky Way's spiral arms.

This four-way perspective gave me quite a positive charge when I first completed it, although it usually needed an explanation before viewers could relate to it. If we could for just one moment become aware of the incredibly awesome place we are living in, the mundane concerns of daily life would lose much of their seeming importance.

WHALE SONG ALONG THE MILKY WAY

16

D. Taylor © 94

Everyone who walks the pathway of life presents a certain quanta of psychic affiliations, not only from the present life, but from a comparatively large number of past lives.

—Ernest L. Norman

Those who cannot remember the past are doomed to repeat it.

—George Santayana

The belief in reincarnation is accepted by more than half the population of our planet, although in the United States this percentage is a much smaller number. Science considers reincarnation unprovable by empirical methods and most Western religions see it as a far-out Eastern philosophy unsupported by Biblical teachings.

Science tells us we can think and reason due to an advanced organization of pulpy matter known as our brain. This biological mechanism, according to science, determines all differences as they are expressed in humankind—good or bad, smart or dumb. Psychology and psychiatric science also describe the human mind and its expression as a relationship of various complexes, mechanisms, and phobias, engendered from procreation and the will to survive.

This brings us to the crux of the matter, which is: What if the mind of a human being was not simply a biological organism formed genetically from some distant primordial ooze, or the product of a hocus-pocus creation set in motion by an almighty white-robed Santa Claus; what if this mind was actually an interdimensional energy system functioning inviolately according to definite natural principles related to the environment through a long series of evolutionary patterns called birth and death. Not a mystical Eastern philosophy, but a true scientific process by which the Universal life force divides itself into finite particles through which this Infinite energy system learns about itself.

FORTUNE FAVORS THE BRAVE

It is one thing to show a man he is in error, and another to put him in possession of truth.
—John Locke

Each particle or human being, having a direct line to the parent source, is limited only by the perceptions of experience formed and contained as energy constructs; instincts, memories, inspirations, etc. This brings us to

MYSTIC ISLES 2

the reason some people are so creatively inspired: simply because they don't have the blocks from past-life traumas influencing their expression, plus the added bias of having already developed their creative abilities in previous lives. They have a clear channel and a strong connection to this Universal source of life, a source everyone is capable of tapping into! There is no magic formula, no special gifts, only natural laws or principles by which all creative manifestation abides. It is quite simple and effortless once the blocks have been removed and the proper mental attitude is established.

Reincarnation, understood as an exact science, explains not only enigmas such as Mozart's mastery of music at age five, but also the destructive tendencies expressed in childhood that later develop into psychopathic killers. While this book is primarily focused on the positive, healthy aspects of inspiration and creative expression, individuals such as Adolph Hitler represent the destructive potential inherent in the human mind; Hitler was "inspired" for strictly self-ish and negative purposes. We all carry with us the negative energies from previous lives, and if left unrecognized, they will continue to poison our minds in the form of selfish, destructive behavior.

My own experience with this concept has been extensive and it has been the greatest help in clearing the channel of my mind so that I could be more receptive to my own creative nature. I can honestly say that until I reached my late twenties, I was a thoroughly blocked-off individual, incapable of being inspired or expressing myself in any creative way. I would have persistent nightmares that upon awakening would carry over into my daily life, leaving me feeling blocked off from any real joy or purpose to my life. I experienced recurring dreams where I would be fighting in wars, killing others and being killed myself over and over again. I began to realize my destructive acts in previous lives had come back to haunt me, but I found myself in a state of denial, unwilling to accept, at first, the reality of my past-life escapades.

SEADREAMS

God the Beautiful is manifest in the
synchronized scenery of nature . . .
His divinity is smiling at us in the flowers.
—Paramahansa Yogananda

The dreams and other psychic phenomena increased in their impact in my life, and I also became aware of positive spiritual forces working with me and helping me to adjust to a more expanded awareness of life, which

REUNION

LADY IN THE CLOUDS

included the realization of having lived thousands of past lives!

I have been an avid reader all my life and read everything from *The Autobiography of a Yogi* by Paramahansa Yogananda to *The Teachings of Don Juan* by Carlos Castaneda; from Buddhism to Christian teachings, and anything metaphysical I could find. But at age twenty-eight I made a discovery in my local library that totally changed my life forever. As I walked down a row in the library that I had somehow missed in the countless times I searched through the books looking for something new and stimulating to read, I felt an invisible hand that seemed to stop me directly in front of a group of books I had never seen before. The first book I picked up was *The Voice of Venus* and as I opened it up, I felt a beautiful upliftment and transcendence flowing into my mind. Truly an

incredible experience that lasted for several months as I read the book! These were the teachings of the Universal Brotherhood of Light, "channeled into" written form by a man named Ernest L. Norman.

I was totally taken up with the power these teachings generated in my life, and a short time later I became a dedicated student and had many earth-shaking psychic experiences. Ruth Norman, also known as Uriel, was the wife of Ernest Norman and publisher of his books through a nonprofit organization. She became my spiritual teacher, a powerhouse of spiritual power and healing energy. On a daily basis, I witnessed incredible psychic phenomena, beautiful healings, and a wondrous spiritual enlightenment that totally boggled my mind in its acceleration and expansion of my consciousness!

. . .Thoughts,
Which ten times faster glide than the Sun's beams.
—William Shakespeare

It was Uriel's encouragement that inspired my creative expressions as I learned how a true Spiritual Master helps bring out the best in her students. Most importantly, I learned to apply in my life the principles of energy as they were described in Ernest and Ruth Norman's teaching curriculum, a library of over one hundred books! I learned about my past and how to remove the blocks of past-life trauma, which is the process involved in developing a better connection with your creative higher self.

As I began to accept my destructive past-life expressions—in one case, as one of the conquistadors responsible for the annihilation of the Inca empire—I experienced incredible healings that left me feeling infused with a new creative energy, which began to express through me in the form of writing and painting. Both of these creative expressions were completely foreign to me, previous to my past-life realizations. But once the blocks of past-life trauma have been removed, the natural process of allowing inspiration to flow through you becomes a joyous adventure, essential in maintaining a healthy alignment with your own higher self or creative nature. To learn to listen to and follow your inner voice is not only essential in developing your creative abilities, but it can save your very life!

Almost everyone has, at one time or another, been rescued from dangerous or dire circumstances by taking direction from their own intuition. When we flip a switch walking into a room, the light goes on, but seldom do we consider the scientific principle that allows the illumination. Just as the light bulb is activated when the circuit to the power plant is completed, so does acting upon our own intuitive guidance connect us to the Powerhouse or Transmitter charging us with the creative energy that interpenetrates and regenerates all life. We become infused with this light and power, and are then able to complete projects that otherwise would seem impossible.

RAINBOW'S END 2

They are ill discoverers that think there is no land, when they can see nothing but water.
—Francis Bacon

Inspiration manifests itself in an infinite variety of ways, yet always follows natural, scientific principles that only seem supernatural or magical because we are ignorant of the cause-and-effect equation that directs all life. We are all capable of developing our creative abilities; it is simply a matter of opening our minds and tapping into the limitless supply of creative power that forms and maintains planets, stars, galaxies, universes—and people!

The natural science that guides the planets in their orbital paths follows the same principles that guide all of us in our endless cycles of birth and death. In our ability to recognize our limitations and rise above them to express creatively, we connect up with the Infinite Intelligence that can and will direct, inspire, and guide us in every aspect of our lives.

DISTANT SHORES 2

The Science of Inspiration

The following was excerpted from a workshop presented by the artist at a Whole Life Expo in Los Angeles, California.

Good day, everyone! What I would like to talk about today is developing self-mastery and expanding your creative nature. A big step in this direction is to realize and understand that our minds are fully capable of attuning to many higher levels of information. In order to attain these higher levels, we have to begin to train ourselves to perceive the negative influences and various blockages that are affecting us, which are the negative traits of our own character. As we recognize these traits, such as selfishness, egomania, and so on, we become more humble.

Humility is a direct hook-up to higher Intelligences living in the spiritual worlds, where light, creativity, and inspiration are amplified in a much greater way than in our world. Such higher worlds are worlds that we can eventually evolve into, as we learn about how people live there and begin to live our own lives in accordance with the way that they live. This doesn't mean that there is some dogmatic approach that you are supposed to use, but just the opposite is true. A true Spiritual Science teaches us how to discard destructive mental attitudes and become progressive in our daily lives.

It is very important that we find spiritual teachings that are compatible with our level of development. This can be different for different people. Follow your inner voice, intuition, or whatever you call it, but continue to expand your knowledge through study, meditation, and all methods and means that help in the enlightenment process.

I personally own a metaphysical library of over one hundred volumes that I have been reading for the past twenty-five years. Reading these books is unique, as it gives me a way of attuning my mind to the perfected Minds that originally channeled the information in them. As I attune to their Minds, I am, in effect, allowing their positive energy to flow into me, and my lower frequency is raised to a certain extent, depending on my efforts and realizations.

We have to do the work necessary in discovering where the blocks are within ourselves. As we do this work, and make that effort, then we begin to receive much greater help from Angelic or intuitive forces, spiritual Brothers and Guides—whatever way you wish to envision them. They are able to help us move ourselves forward in our own spiritual progression.

I have broken down these rather complex and abstract ideas into a simple set of suggestions that can be very beneficial in our efforts to attain self-mastery. These mental excercises were passed on to me by my inner Teachers and Guides, and have been extremely helpful in my personal struggles to attain peace of mind. I feel certain that if you will take these ideas to heart, you will gain the benefit from them, but of course this can only take place through your own efforts and desire for self-improvement.

Seven Ways To Help Raise Your Consciousness

1. Keep a Positive Attitude

Fill your life with concern for others and work on developing and expressing your creative abilities.

2. Learn To Be Patient with Yourself

"Rome was not built in a day." It has taken thousands of years to create your present-life conditions. Give yourself plenty of time to unravel the mystery of past-life associations and the methods and means of attaining self-mastery.

3. Be Persistent

It will take effort on your part to attain what you aspire to. Your continued efforts will determine your success in reaching your objectives, in whatever manner you have chosen.

All rising to a great place is by a winding stair.

—Francis Bacon

4. Let Spirit Work with You

The energy that is the activating force and substance of the Universe is an Infinite Creative Intelligence which will regenerate

THE LEARNING LIGHT

your consciousness. Progression or regression is the choice we make daily by our thoughts, actions, and deeds.

5. Lighten Up

Keep your sense of humor and do not let temporary problems get you down. Laughter has healing properties.

6. Extend the Boundaries of Your Mind

Begin the study of consciousness. Use your intuition to find books, audio tapes, and video tapes that inspire and stimulate your spiritual growth, and recognize that you are an eternal, evolutionary, spiritual being. Life and death are simply doorways into opposite sides of the great cyclic movement of consciousness.

7. Raise your awareness through self analysis; learn to spot the clues to past-life memories:

A. *Note your special rapport and reactions to people places, and things, such as*
- historical figures
- religious leaders
- artists and art décor
- clothing, food, homes, vacation spots, sports, hobbies, etc.
- epic movies and plays

B. *Look closely at personal, emotional crises*
- physical problems
- disturbing dreams
- psychological problems
- fears and anxieties
- negative family or personal relationships
- work-related problems

C. *Analyze your belief structures*
- Be open to new concepts that are in advance of dogmatic practices and beliefs.
- Learn to question your attitudes and opinions. Fixed attitudes, opinions, and beliefs generate an obsessive and narrow focus of life. They cripple your ability to function with logic and reason.

[Questions & Answers]

Student: How do you account for people who seem to be highly attuned and creatively inspired, yet they are also egomaniacs?

Teacher: What happens in cases of that nature is that you can be in tune with your spiritual self and be bringing in totally inspired works, yet if you are selfish and possessive of the inspired expressions, you are slowly severing the connection to the higher self and will eventually lose touch with the source of your inspiration. We must keep in mind that whatever work you are doing, if truly inspired, it is coming from the higher intelligent Minds who are totally humble and are fully aware of the principles of the Infinite. The main point being, that this Infinite Intelligence is functioning according to the basic principle of selflessness, as it is recreating the sum and total of everything in the universe, including our lives.

It is very foolish to think we can live selfishly and still be able to maintain our attunement with the vast Creative Cosmos which is totally selfless in its expression. We would be diametrically opposed to this most basic principle. So such people as you described, will eventually realize that egotism and selfishness will not help them to progress on the spiritual pathway, and this recognition will be a great lesson to them in the future. This is a lesson that all of us must eventually learn as we become more in tune with our spiritual selves and our progressive evolution. Does that answer your question?

Student: Yes, I believe it does.

Teacher: Now the second part of your question was, how do we remove the blocks keeping us from expressing creatively? It is important that we begin to look at ourselves very honestly. We must take complete responsibility for our lives and learn to see adversity and problems as positive lessons. No matter how negative the circumstances may seem, as we are able to turn it around and see that—let's say, you get punched in the nose—instead of losing control emotionally, you could gain a great lesson by not giving in to the reaction of wanting to strike back.

In Nature you behold the mother aspect of God full of gentleness, tenderness, and kindness.

—Paramahansa Yogananda

I realize this is a difficult situation to keep your mental balance in, but we could use the example of what Jesus said about turning the other cheek.

SUNSET SERENITY

He didn't mean that when someone comes up and punches you on one side that you turn the other side and let him punch you on that side, too. What he meant was that when someone is projecting a negative energy in your direction, you don't allow yourself to get pulled down into that low, reactionary state of mind. That lower state of mind is in direct opposition to the balance that we should be striving to maintain in relationship with our higher spiritual self. We should become aware that we are creating our future by our acts of today. This is a very important principle that will positively change our life if we really abide by its connotations.

Student: What if someone is giving you bad vibes or says something negative to you, what would you do?

Teacher: That is part of developing self-mastery to where you no longer allow yourself to be so strongly influenced by the exterior circumstances of what is taking place in your life. If I were driving by and saw two people punching each other out, it's going to tune me in to some negative circumstances from my past. In my past lives I used to like to fight; it was part of my heritage.

But we have to learn how to master our own thoughts so that we don't allow ourselves to get pulled into that negative situation.

Because we know now that we are a spiritual being, the energies that you allow to move through your consciousness, as stated earlier, are creating your future.

If someone is out there projecting negative energy, that is a very hard lesson that they will have to learn someday. They are basically creating a hell for themselves; not that there is a hell and a heaven, but your mind and your thought processes, what you have been able to understand and establish as your reality, that is the mental atmosphere you are going to live in. If your mind has been actively attuned to a more positive expres-

sion, then you are going to find yourself living in a more positive world. There will be people living on that higher level helping you to learn how to live progressively, looking towards the future of an even more elevated state.

On the negative side of this duality of consciousness, you can also get pulled down easily if you allow yourself to sympathize with those people who are still living in the dark, with no interest in spiritual development.

Ultimately, we must realize that everyone is traveling along their own pathway of life, and their life experience is every bit as important to them as our path is to us. It should always be our greatest goal to find our connection with our spiritual self so that guidance can lead us away from negative situations. I personally have been saved five or six times from what could have been fatal accidents, by my own intuition; oftentimes it was almost without my consent. I needed to be knocked on the head with a sledge hammer to get my attention and wake me up to the fact that something bad was going to happen, and I have a positive mission to carry out.

Everyone does have a mission, and the mission is to learn enough about life to where you can move yourself into a more positive relationship with your own spiritual self, which will establish your pathway towards a progressive evolution of consciousness.

Student: I have a question about creativity and inspiration. I have found the creativity part comes very easily but the problem is in marketing or making a living with it, therefore, not being able to do it on a full-time basis and eventually having to go back to working a so-called "real job." How do you make a living from creativity and inspiration?

Teacher: I can give myself as an example. I have been an artist for about thirteen years. I have experienced a certain amount of so-called

In her (Nature's) inventions nothing is lacking, and nothing is superfluous.
                    —Leonardo da Vinci

THE SPIRIT OF MOTHER NATURE

One day my paintings shall be worth more than the price of the paint.

—Vincent Van Gogh

material success (a very small amount). I am also a carpenter, and that is how I have made my living. So I am not going to quit my day job and throw my hammer away. Keep some means of supporting yourself so you can continue the creative process without becoming stressed out over financial problems. It's different for everyone, as you have to know when it is time to take that step to where you are more committed to your own creative expression. There have been many artists in the past who could not give their paintings away while they were alive—such as Vincent Van Gogh—yet today his artwork sells for millions of dollars per painting! When we are dead, perhaps our artwork will be worth something; until then, I wouldn't put a lot of importance on it.

It is important to do it, however, because it is an attunement to your spiritual self that is really the point. It doesn't matter if you are materially successful, either in wealth or fame. Look at your creative inspirations as a kind of incredible therapy in developing peace of mind, and if there is material success, consider that the icing on the cake.

Student: I was asked to do some art for a celebration during Thanksgiving. I just had fun with it and didn't take it too seriously. Is this the way to let inspiration flow?

Teacher: Yes, that is an excellent point, because there are so many artists who have such over-inflated egos. It is because they are really insecure about themselves and they see themselves in competition with other artists, so they feel the need to push themselves out in front of everyone else.

What you are talking about is very important because inspiration comes to us as free creative energy, so we must see ourselves simply as channels who are being given an opportunity to express art and inspiration as a means of helping others. Art is a great way of learning about yourself and taking those important initial steps in developing self-mastery, which is the only true pathway to gaining peace of mind. We must break down our ego so it is not dominating our expression, and learn to allow our spiritual self to overshadow our life and creatively inspire us. Thus we will be learning the science of inspiration.

Student: What if the inspiration comes and goes and you can't turn it off?

Teacher: When it comes and you can't turn it off, don't try to turn it off. Just let it flow! I recall one time when I had three weeks off work and I was in tune with painting very strongly. All I did was paint for three weeks, and I ended up completing six different paintings. Some of them are on the greeting cards that you see on display up here. The cycle was in for this creative inspiration to just flow, and flow, and flow. While I was painting, it seemed that I had stepped into this other room that was being illuminated with this pure light and radiant energy of creative inspiration, and my entire psychic was being recharged with this great power! As I completed this series of paintings, it was as if it was just shut off.

This is the challenge oftentimes for artists; Vincent Van Gogh had this problem. As he would raise himself up into this beautiful creative state of mind, where this inspiration was flowing so rapidly, and he would complete the work and come back to the reality of the unhappy life he was living, a manic-depressive state of mind would consume him. I have experienced this same negative condition myself, and have had a very difficult time balancing the positive and negative elements of my own nature.

Interpretation is the revenge of the intellect on art.

—Susan Sontag

This is a very important principle to realize, in that we have this duality of consciousness. We have this higher, positive self that is attempting to guide us into our own more positive future, and we have a lower self that is a product of the past. We have to let go of preconceived ideas of who we are. As we let go, and dump out that baggage from the past, we become much lighter and more able to rise up into that frequency where that higher spiritual consciousness is constantly functioning and radiating out its own creative expression into our lives.

ASCENSION OF THE SPIRIT SHIP

Imagination is more important than knowledge.

—Albert Einstein

SUNSET STALLIONS

UFOs in Art

My suspicion is that the universe is not only stranger than we suppose, but stranger than we can suppose.

—J.B.S. Haldane

The UFO phenomenon has generated tremendous interest in our present day, although it is still treated as a taboo subject and generally not accepted as legitimate subject matter for artists. Inspiring one of the greatest mysteries of our time, surely many artists are communicating visionary statements relating their own unique and powerful experiences directly associated with UFOs and their extraterrestrial occupants.

Imagine a civilization that has been evolving positively for millions of years, a society based upon an advanced scientific development that integrates technology and spiritual awareness in a synthesis of pure creative expression. They would live in a paradise that would be impossible for us to conceive because the minds of the inhabitants of these extraterrestrial worlds have been purified of all lower, negative, emotional thoughts. They carry no weapons, only love in their hearts, their main purpose in life being to explore the universe and help those people in lesser states of development to awaken to their true spiritual nature.

As we continue to explore the universe and become awestruck and humbled by the magnitude of it all, we no doubt will come to accept our planet as one of countless worlds given the opportunity to progress, and eventually take our place in the peaceful brotherhood of planets along the Milky Way.

SHUTTLE TO MISSION CONTROL: NOTHING UNUSUAL TO REPORT

*West of these out to seas colder than
        the Hebrides I must go
Where the fleet of stars is anchored
and the young star captains glow.*
                —James Elvoy Flecker

PLEIADEAN PARADISE

My UFO Experience

Space isn't remote at all. It's only an hour's drive away if your car could go straight up.
—Sir Fred Hoyle

The first question that arises about the UFO phenomenon is subjective: Do you or do you not believe in the reality of extraterrestrial life? To my knowledge, there is no concrete, physical evidence to prove that we are being visited, yet national polls have indicated that half of all Americans—well over 100 million people— believe that extra- terrestrial intelligence does exist. Personal experience is certainly the greatest validation of belief, yet is gener- ally difficult, if not impossible, to prove to a skeptical, closed- minded individual.

My own personal close encounter inside a starship falls into this category. I was given an incredible, illuminating, never-to- be-forgotten contact aboard a starship in 1978 when traveling in the Caribbean islands. I had no previous interest in UFOs, although I was open to the idea and at the time studying and reading about the many different concepts of metaphysics.

INTERPLANETARY TRAVELERS

One night, after a good day surfing in the sparkling clear Caribbean waters, I lay down on my bed to go to sleep. Before falling unconscious, I began to feel a very unusual spinning sensation. It felt as if my entire body was gyrating in countless cyclic pat- terns—a very unusual and stimulating sensation. As my mind began to clear after this experience, I suddenly became aware of myself standing inside what I assumed was some type of spacecraft.

Incredulous with my present situation I received a mental greeting.

A teacher affects eternity; he can never tell where his influence stops.

—Henry James

"Yes, friend, you are truly with us. Now allow your mind to relax, and we will be most happy to shed some light on your present predicament . . . "

My mind was reeling in the most tremendous state of mental excitement and anticipation I had ever experienced! The surroundings in which I found myself were pulsating with a brilliant luminosity that was literally emanating from everywhere about me. And here, directly in front of me, was a group of seven beings, both male and female, standing around and manipulating what appeared to be some sort of control panel.

One particular soul, human in appearance and dressed in a pure

DISTANT SHORES

white space suit, was looking at me with the most intense, penetrating eyes I had ever seen. He seemed to be able to pierce directly into my mind—and I knew this was no "human being," in my normal frame of conception. There was a beautiful glow surrounding all of these beings and I noticed such a warmth and tremendous sense of peace that was in stark contrast to the absolute excitement I felt as I began to truly realize: I was standing inside a starship from

some distant planet! Again my lighted host directed his thoughts into my mind, and I calmed down a little.

"Please feel comfortable, my friend, as we are your brothers and wish only to make you feel at ease, so that you may gain some benefit from this encounter.

In the Universe the difficult things are done as if they were easy.

—Lucretius

INTERGALACTIC EXPRESS

"You are one of many that we are contacting in this way, so as to let our presence be known upon your Earth—to prepare the people for the future plan that is beginning to unfold. I can see that your mind is bursting forth with questions, but please relax and I will attempt to answer your queries.

"Your people of planet Earth have yet to realize that intelligent life is teeming, virtually throughout the universe, in advanced civilizations and levels of development that would completely defy description. The countless billions of stars that appear in your astronomer's telescopes are only a fraction of the overall magnitude of Infinite Creation—a

Creation that had no beginning nor will there ever be an ending, as all worlds, stars, and even galaxies function in the orderly pattern of cyclic regeneration.

"We come from a planet outside your solar system, the name of which would mean nothing to you.

"As you can see, our craft is formed from a crystalline material that seems to sparkle and glow, emanating a soft but brilliant, phosphorescent-like illumination. This material is actually similar to your diamond, only in a highly refined form with certain electromagnetic properties of which your most advanced scientists are unaware.

What we have learned is like a handful of earth; what we have yet to learn is like the whole world.

—Avviayar

SIGHTING OVER SEDONA

"In the center of our cylindrical craft, you will notice a tube-like configuration that runs vertically through our starship. In this tube, you see a brilliant, pulsating, golden substance that is fluctuating iridescently in the various colors of the prismatic spectrum; this is the heart of our propulsion system. Through a process that would be difficult for you to understand, a sort of generating device begins an oscillation with this brilliant substance. It is actually a light plasma that polarizes our craft in a positive to negative phase-reversal pattern; in other words, the electromagnetic properties of this plasma regenerate into an intense, high-frequency condition. This begins a chain reaction in which the entire atomic structure of the craft is now vibrating in harmonic resonance with this initial chain reaction. Our starship is no longer subject to the physical laws of gravity, momentum, and inertia, as we have passed beyond that particular frequency spectrum.

"In a way you could say that our ship is propelled by light radiation, although it is a much higher frequency than the visible light spectrum. So we travel on the electromagnetic radiation bands that crisscross throughout the cosmos, and only when we get to our particular destination or planet do we again change our craft back to its more gross, atomic form. Then, through a simple magnetic process of attraction and repulsion, do we land or depart from any particular point . . . "

*The real voyage of discovery consists not in
seeking new landscapes but in having new eyes.*
—Marcel Proust

My mind was staggering under the excitement of the mental discourse I was receiving; yet, in my heightened state of awareness, I seemed to understand the knowledge that was being imparted to me. With his eyes sparkling mischievously, my guide continued his elucidations.

"I can see in your thoughts that you feel you can comprehend the workings of our starship; but please realize, I am speaking directly into your mind, your mental self, so the more primitive elements of your nature are being set aside for the time being. And rest assured, Friend, that there is much, MUCH to learn and experience, and we should never feel that we know it all, as this will block the path for future knowledge.

CLOSE ENCOUNTER AT DOLPHINS' COVE

"The workings of our starship function according to certain principles that could be likened to the very movement of Creation itself. As all energy moves in waveform patterns, so do the countless thoughts that course through your mind move and function in this same manner and way. What to you appears to be fantastic or unbelievable, to us is a reality that we have included in our own particular

All our science measured against reality, is primitive and childlike and yet it is the most precious thing we have.

—Albert Einstein

CELESTIAL COVE

realizations and concepts. As you see us as fantastic beings, bordering on the limits of your imagination, in actuality we are humble participants—riding the life stream and helping our brothers in lesser states of awareness to awaken to their true nature. We are truly brothers to humanity, and are looking forward to the near future, when your people can accept us and desire us to land our spacecraft on your planet's floor, so that you, too, can join with us as working members of this great Cosmic Mind."

As I had been listening intently for about fifteen minutes to this incredible mental discourse, I now found myself losing my grasp on the heightened and elevated state of mind I was so enjoying up until now. As I looked at these beautiful, radiant beings standing in front of me, projecting such a serenity and sense of peace, and at the same time a truly advanced intelligence, I began to feel very primitive in comparison. I was like a savage in the jungle in relation to these benevolent beings, and my mind rapidly sank into the pits of self-pity and depression.

As I looked up at the Brother who had been communicating with me up until now, I saw him glance over at one of the female crew members, who now looked directly into my eyes.

PLIEADEAN PARADISE 2

We, too, once lived in this house of stars . . .
—Murmurs of Earth

I stood transfixed, looking into the eyes of the most beautiful, angelic woman I had ever seen. I literally felt a beam of pure, loving compassion surge into the depths of my being, immediately lifting me up again into the positive elevated state of mind I had initially experienced!

I knew then that these advanced, extraterrestrial beings did not judge me according to my limited belief system of comparisons. They were only interested in my own benefit and welfare.

Again I felt the mental prompting of my host, who I assumed to be the captain: "Now Friend, we must return you to your proper location and bid you adieu . . ."

"Please wait! Can I go with you?!"

"No, Friend. Our world would be impossible to you. But rest assured, with your dedicated efforts to integrate yourself into this great plan, you may someday come with us . . .

"May the Light of the Infinite Creative Intelligence always guide your footsteps; farewell until a future time."

I once again felt the unusual, gyrating and spinning sensation I'd felt at the beginning of my encounter, and I found myself fully awake, lying on my bed, with a crystal-clear memory of everything that had just tran-

INTERSTELLAR VOYAGER

spired. I felt sure I had just experienced an actual encounter with extraterrestrial beings.

As I now reflect back on this experience, some sixteen years later, I feel very fortunate to have been contacted in this way. It was not long after this encounter on the Caribbean island of Puerto Rico that I began having many psychic experiences that shook me loose from many of the limited and rigid thought patterns that, for the most part, are all based on the fear of the unknown. I began allowing myself to be guided more and more

TEMPLE CITY

I don't think we are in Kansas anymore, Toto.
—Dorothy, "The Wizard of Oz"

by my own intuition. At age thirty, having never painted or been involved in creative expression of any kind, I awoke one morning with the desire to draw a starship. I began to feel a beautiful, uplifting transcendence every time I sat down to paint. I now consider artistic expression to be a large part of my life's work.

I have related my UFO experience to thousands of people in the past sixteen years, on television and radio shows, and I have encountered many skeptics, some very hostile. But every time I have an opportunity to relate my experience, I again feel the beautiful, transcending state of mind that has become so familiar to me in the many years since my original encounter, and I know the truth will someday be made known . . .

The lost civilization of Atlantis, long the subject of myth and conjecture, is depicted in the following two paintings. Lost but not forgotten, the ancient ruins lie hidden, deep beneath the sparkling, blue-green waters of the Atlantic Ocean.

Some researchers believe that the civilization of Atlantis was actually initiated by an advanced race of spiritually enlightened space travelers from a group of seven stars known as the Pleiades. The mythology of many cultures, relating of Gods descending from the stars, is traced back to this star cluster which is in the constellation Taurus.

Although six or seven bright stars are detectable to the human eye, the Pleiades are made up of several hundred, which are about four hundred light years distant from Earth. Grecian scholars of ancient times talk specifically about Atlantis, and Atlas, who was an Atlantian, descended from the great Gods who came from the Pleiades. North American Indians tell of white beings of exceptional beauty and intelligence who were godlike and helped to resolve crises in the lives of their forefathers. In folklore, the Mayans of southern Mexico are said to have descended to Earth from the Pleiades.

Atlantis at its zenith is thought to have contained seven major cities, which were built and patterned after cities from the Pleiadean planets. These advanced Spiritual Teachers shared their knowledge and wisdom with the Earth people, only to watch in the latter days the destruction of this island paradise.

Today, many strange stories are told of unusual phenomena credited to an area known as the Bermuda Triangle in the Atlantic Ocean. It is thought by some psychics and sensitives that these phenomena are related to a damaged power-tower crystal that still oscillates with the electromagnetic spectrum of the earth. The imbalance creates energy surges that wreak havoc upon those caught within the force field. This advanced technology, when in proper balance, produced virtually free energy for this once-great civilization, where interplanetary travel was common knowledge, and the Atlanteans lived a seemingly heavenly existence, both above and below the water.

THE GUARDIANS OF ATLANTIS

We are stardust
We are golden
And we've got to get ourselves
Back to the garden
—Joni Mitchell

RETURN TO ATLANTIS

A Word From the Author-Artist

A new scientific truth does not triumph by convincing its opponents to see the light, but rather because its opponents eventually die, and a new generation grows up that is familiar with it.

—Max Planck

In describing my experiences in this book, I realize that much of the information could be termed visionary, imaginary, or even the ramblings of some lunatic having psychotic episodes. In fact, I have been called the latter by some skeptics and critics. To this I reply that the work speaks for itself and I simply consider myself the channel, not the voice of God or the Devil but somewhere in between, where intuition manifests as an inner voice guiding me on my own personal pathway of spiritual awakening.

Everyone has this inner voice although it speaks to each in their own personal manner, dependent on the experiences that have formed the reality in which they live. I respect their position and realize that, although we may disagree, we have the responsibility of being tolerant of all people's viewpoints. It is in this tolerance that we can break down the barriers of ignorance that separate our world's populations into armed camps, dangerously paranoid of ideas and beliefs that disagree with our own.

Much of the destructive and violent behavior that is so prevalent in our society is the expression of minds that are lost in the darkness of ignorance, unwilling to take responsibility for their situation. I was one of these lost souls, but even as I struggled to free myself, I only became more entangled by the restrictive attitudes of selfishness and egotism. "I once was lost but now I am found," to quote the words from the famous song. I found myself, my spiritual creative

nature which has guided me out of the darkness into the light.

Channeling is a word that has become quite common in the new-age vocabulary, and although I do describe my understanding of this process somewhat in this book, I feel it needs more explanation—especially in regard to my personal experiences as they are related and recorded in these writings.

The readings and channeled articles in this book were received in what at first seems to be a fantastic, outrageous, or even an unbelievable method. I can understand such skepticism, as I couldn't believe it myself at first. In fact, my first attempts left me freaking out at what seemed to be a terrifying and bizarre experience. The method I used was to sit down with a microphone and a tape recorder and, closing my eyes, simply speak the train of thoughts as they came to my mind. There was no preparation, and what at first seemed strange and terrifying became quite natural and normal as I continued this process over many years.

It seemed the channeled information was coming from some vast transmitter and I was just tuning the receiver of my mind into the thought streams that would be spoken by me onto the recording tape. I do not claim that this information is the word of God, or that it is one hundred percent accurate, or even that it is coming from some higher form of intelligence, although I do most often get positive feedback and validation from those who receive these readings. I make no claims of supernatural or spirit influences but simply carry on in the way that I feel intuitively guided.

My experiences with art and painting are of a similar nature.

Oftentimes when channeling painting, writing, or voice recording, the intense power could be felt literally flowing through my mind and body like electric currents. All the senses are stepped up and amplified a thousand fold compared to my normal expression. Incredibly beautiful sensations of peace and unconditional love seemed to flow through my mind onto the canvas or into the writing or in whatever creative expression I was involved.

I must say, though, that this channelship that I have been developing was not instantaneous nor was it easy to believe and accept as reality. It has only been through many years of hard work and dedication that this process has been developed. It is a continuous and never-ending vigilance that is necessary to keep the channeled information from being tainted by the hidden motivations of selfishness and egomania of the channel.

I feel certain that these efforts of self-introspection will be necessary for the remainder of my life, although it makes sense that anything of any real value comes to us only through unceasing effort and dedication to our goal.

We are all channels on some level, and it will always be our choice whether to soar with the Eagles, brave and free, or to grovel in the muddy, slime-infested swamps of our many fears and insecurities. Let us awaken from the long sleep of self-imposed limitations and ignorance, and like the chrysalis, transform ourselves into the brilliant butterfly, and flying free, spread our pollen of unconditional love to all who will so partake!

*The clearest way into the Universe is through
a forest wilderness.*

—John Muir

NATURE'S PATH

Principles and Practice of Past Life Therapy

All great truths begin as blasphemies.
—George Bernard Shaw

The following was presented at the Learning Light Foundation in Anaheim, California, by the author-artist, through whom members of the Universal Brotherhood are speaking to the class—first providing information about higher spiritual worlds and later supplying individual, past-life readings.

Brothers: "Good evening again, friends, and fellow travelers on the pathway of Spirit, which is leading you onto that spiraling stairway into the stars.

"The stars may seem very distant, very isolated, and yet would you believe the entire physical universe is a combination of vast amounts of energies that are functioning as part of a group consciousness—a Cosmic Mind within which we are each a cell! The turning of the planet in the four different motions in which your Earth is moving is not by chance! These things are all a part of a great plan, a great Cosmic Consciousness, and it is but to see from the inner side of life that these truths become evident.

"From the limited perspective of the person standing on the surface of the planet looking up, they can either see the fear and insecurity of the unknown, or the challenge of the future. The future is always the next step we take in which the doors of perception open up into an entirely new state of consciousness. This is basically how spiritual progression takes place as we constantly select the direction we are moving in, which is either progressively into the future, or backwards into the past. The stream of consciousness is a two-way river—a river that is flowing in a circular motion, spiraling into the more positively-biased evolutionary progression, and also recycling the negative side of this motion into positive energies that can again be reinstated into a healthy relationship with this Infinite Creative Intelligence."

(A train blows its horn loudly as it passes close by.)

"This is a noisy world! Can you imagine a world in which there is no noise at all, where the audible sound is simply an attunement to what we could call the music of the spheres? A place of continuous peace and serenity, incredible beauty and illumination? These are the worlds we have described to you as being those future levels of life to which you can attain. It has been called 'heaven,' but again we reiterate, it is not so much a location as it is a state of mind. These heaven worlds will take you out of the morass and the heavy-handed consciousness of the material world, and you can ascend into the pure, finer, altruistic conditions in a world where love and brotherhood are the mainstay of the people's lives.

"This love is based upon scientific principles by which each individual has developed a sense of attunement with their creative nature. In establishing this plus-positive attunement, they are not allowing themselves to be pulled down and away from this higher-frequency relationship. They have become very selective in their thought processes. This positive attunement is the only difference between those individuals living in a lower world and those living in a higher world. Of course, 'lower' and 'higher' are very much relative to the state of mind of each person. One person's floor is another person's ceiling!

"For those of you who are here tonight, we Brothers are aware that you are making those steps forward, to whatever degree you have dedicated yourself, to a future which will be free of many of the limitations which are presently affecting you. And to your dedicated efforts in overcoming your past, we wish to bow humbly and wish you Godspeed in your quest for spiritual attainment.

"As you should know by now, this quest has taken you up and down many roads, for many hundreds or thousands of lifetimes, with many detours. Oftentimes you became lost in some of the darker regions of life. At times you became stranded in a past life on the barrier reef of some regressive lifestyle which was simply the inability to move mentally beyond the limitations of the physical consciousness.

"This is, in essence, the nature of the population of your planet, where everyone is functioning for the most part based on their desires for the material world and its many sensual gratifications. There are a number of individuals, such as yourselves, who have peered beyond these limitations and have begun to take those steps, which are the sometimes seemingly perilous journey into the psychic world. Yet this world is derived from what we can call the psychic centers, the chakras of the *psychic anatomy* which are opening up, similar to a flower as it reaches full bloom and emanates the wondrous fragrance of its own spiritual nature. As these psychic centers are stimulated and recognized as a spiritual awakening, your life will never be the same. It is the road to true freedom!

"These chakras are the fourth-dimensional energy centers that are precipitating the energies from the psychic body into the physical body, and thus this linkage is the only thing that keeps you alive in a physical world. If you lose this linkage with any part of this psychic anatomy, the physical body will then suffer and eventually lose its life force. This psychic body is simply a vessel into which the consciousness of spirit has been poured, and this vessel takes on the shape of whatever that individual has built for himself or herself out of experience. Thus, this shape is based on the understanding and mental perception that each individual has established as a reality. We all create our own heaven or hell—which is simply a state of mind, not an actual place or location.

"We are describing the principles of spiritual progression as a means of helping those people who are interested in stepping onto a higher plateau. This will allow them to see clearly and elevate themselves above and beyond the smog-laden, drug-infested atmosphere of the lower earth and astral worlds. The minds of those people living in these lower levels cannot be focused on the crystal-clear pictures of the spiritual worlds; their minds are full of static, similar to the television when it is in between stations, and this static is the lack of integration and attunement with the transmitting source, which in this case we are referring to as the psychic anatomy.

"When anyone has developed an opening within the conduit of his or her mind, the higher intelligence can flow through in an intuitive manner. This channel is not the main instigator of the information but as we previously made the analogy of the television set, again this serves as a good example, as the channel is simply allowing his vessel to be used as the receiver of the higher-frequency stations. Thus through this scientific process, the information can be brought through, both in pictures and words, relative to the individual's past lives. The sub-channel then relates it in the form of these readings. In the student's understanding of this information, and in utilizing the principles of cancellation, the healing of the negative, past-life experience is initiated. Each one can then develop a much greater understanding of who he or she is.

"To 'know thyself' was the chief and basic dictum of Socrates, and it still stands as the most important factor in your spiritual development. To know yourself means learning about the past, because we are all products of the past. Our goal is to learn how to disengage our channel selector from that lower frequency and change it to the higher-frequency channels of our own future, which is always existing potentially in the present moment. The ever present is where the changes can be made and the negative past can be rectified.

The Psychic Anatomy

which is commonly known as the Soul is

A Fourth-Dimensional Energy System

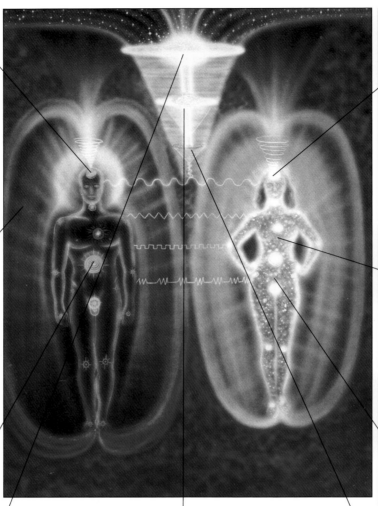

The Brain is a receiver and NOT the thinking mechanism of man! The true transmitter and generating source is the Psychic Anatomy.

The Aura is an electromagnetic field that radiates several feet from the body. It does not contain the full energy information of the true brain, the Psychic Anatomy.

The Chakras are the energy centers that serve as a sprinkler system distributing cosmic energy from the Psychic Anatomy.

Experiences reside as energy vortexes in the Psychic Anatomy. All people have gained positive experiences in their relationship to higher-dimensional spiritual worlds.

Shocks and traumas from past lives exist as aberrations in the Psychic Anatomy.

Present life "memories" are stored in the Psychic Anatomy as energy impulses.

The Psychic Anatomy is an energy system which carries the complete accumulated experiences gained over a period of many lifetimes. It exists in a higher dimension that is not perceptible by the five physical senses, yet it is the true transmitting source, giving life to the physical anatomy. The Psychic Anatomy consists of three interrelated parts:

The Superconsciousness
The Superconsciousness is formed from all of the positive learning experiences, which are in harmony with the Infinite, Creative Intelligence or God. It exists in a higher dimension and is the basic sustaining force for the Psychic Anatomy.

The Mental-Consciousness
The Mental-Consciousness is created from all experiences gained from the sum and total of one's previous lifetimes. The Akashic records reside as energy wave forms in this section of the Psychic Anatomy.

The Subconsciousness
The Subconsciousness solely contains present-life experiences or memories from birth.

"You do not need to continue the negative conditions that translate into the diseases, mental sclerosis, calamities, and accidents, all of the various negative convolutions that seem to happen to you with no rhyme or reason, which are products of cyclic regenerations from past-life associations.

"With this brief introduction, as always we will open the class up to questions and answers that we hope will be helpful to you as students on this pathway of Light.

"Larry, do you have a question?"

Larry: "Yes. Seven years ago my daughter passed away from a brain tumor. It was a very painful period for me but it brought me into an interest in spiritual things, and I wondered what karmic relationship there might have been between my daughter and myself?"

Brothers: "Do you have recognition of your thoughts and emotions at that time, when you first realized your daughter was going to die? What were those feelings?"

Larry: "Helplessness. And after she passed away, a numbness. She received treatments and went into remission for a while, then she started getting worse."

Brothers: "Yes, Larry, we can help you to understand the full picture, as you have taken many pieces of the puzzle and have tried to arrange them on the board in an effort to understand how this event could take place. In this process of introspection, you have become much more interested in learning about your spiritual nature. This is a very positive factor in your life now, but do not misconstrue this as something that should be a hobby; that it is something in which you are gaining information about life that will be to your benefit.

"It will be to your benefit, but there has to be a stronger and stronger conviction of the importance of your spiritual development. You have taken that big step in desiring to know the reasons why you are here—the purpose of your life.

"We can very easily move into the past and take you back to a time in England, in which the various hospitals and doctors were quite primitive. This is back in the early 1700s. There was no real knowledge of how disease was spread, especially diseases such as the plague. There were different periods of time when devastating plagues overran the countries of Europe; in one of these destructive periods, over one quarter of the entire population of Europe was destroyed. This we believe was called the Black Death in the early 1400s.

"We can see your daughter as a doctor, a male, as women were not allowed to be doctors at this particular time. He worked out of a large manor house that also served as the hospital. At this time, the plague began to spread throughout England and was taking a great negative toll on the populations of the cities. You, at that time in this past we are relating, were the brother of the doctor, who is your daughter in your present life. And you both worked together, although you were not a doctor but you had certain business associations in the mercantile business and when you had the time, you worked with your brother. You helped each other take care of the many people who came to you for various ailments.

"The great pestilence, the plague that had devastated some of the eastern European countries, was brought to England by the merchant seamen who had brought back the rats that were infested with the fleas that carried the disease. Today this is known as the bubonic plague. There was a great terror that manifested and became the experience at that time, as the people had no knowledge of how this disease was spread.

"Your daughter, being your brother at that time, was attempting to do anything he could to lessen the pain of the people who were dying of this disease. The patients would become feverish and within three days, they would die with 'buboes,' which was the swelling of the lymph nodes in the groin, and this is how it got the name bubonic plague.

His bliss is older than the sun
Silent and straight the waters run
The lights, the cries, the willows dim
And the dark tide are one with him

—Rupert Brook

"Your own position at this time was that you did not feel that you could be of help in the awful situation that was taking place. You were fortunate in being able to take one of the merchant ships that you had used in your business, and you moved to another part of the country; you moved toward the northern latitudes, up near Norway. The plague had not reached there yet because of the cold weather

SECRET PASSAGE

that killed the fleas that carried the disease. You had escaped the disease but your brother, being a humanitarian, continued to help the many people that were dying around him and he eventually contracted the disease himself. It was a painful, agonizing death in which eventually the spirit was released and freed.

"The belief at that time was that the soul would elevate into the heavens according to the holiness the individual had experienced in his or her relationship with the church or with the church officials. Of course, this was and is not the way spiritual progression takes place. The scar that your daughter incepted was one that created a great dysfunction in the psychic body. In that the brain suffered delirium, and the nervous system was over-heated, the connection between the brain and the psychic body was short-circuited, which planted the seed for the re-expression of the negative wave form structures in your daughter's present-life experience.

"Now you have in a sense come back to work out and overcome the guilt that you felt for having left your brother behind. You made the move that saved your life, as there was nothing you could have done at that time. The brain structures of your brother became aberrant in the connection with the psychic body, which was the actual impingement of the wave forms structures in the brain which were disassociated from the healthy connection with the higher self. This was a time when you were pulled back together, as relatives oftentimes incarnate together over long periods of time. The names and faces may change, but the psychic body retains and re-expresses the information that was and is recorded as blocks, traumas, and diseased conditions. Your daughter reattuned to this past in watching a program on television, and thus the aberrant energies that were in a sense quiescent were focused and established again into her life and began this cancerous condition.

"The best way you can help your daughter is to continue developing your spiritual nature.

Don't allow yourself to be pulled down with the guilt you may feel about a loved one's death, but stand strong in your faith that life is continuous. Death is simply a change from one state of consciousness to another, and as you grow in understanding of Spirit, your daughter will also benefit from your own overcoming of the past.

"Are there any other questions about this lifetime?"

Larry: "None that I can think of. When she passed away, I felt a profound sense of guilt and still do, and it isn't something to feel guilty about, but I sometimes feel it."

Brothers: "Those are the energies you had felt at that specific time. When you reattuned to this past, you knew that you could save yourself but your brother would not come with you. Your daughter was and is a very beautiful soul and gave her life trying to help others.

"The principles of Spirit are inviolate. Everyone is a product of their own experience and in learning the principles of cancellation of negative, past-life experiences, you can eventually heal any diseased condition of the mind or body.

"Leslie, did you have a question?"

Leslie: "Yes, I do. My question is concerning my daughter and her relationship with her father. I have a desire to interfere in their relationship, to counteract his influence over her. He has a very negative influence on her and I want to protect her from that. Something tells me to allow her to go through this relationship so she doesn't have to go through it again in another lifetime. She can maybe break away from him on her own, but I'm concerned for her safety."

Brothers: "We can just reiterate what you just described, which is the basis for each one to realize, that they have the knowledge within themselves, intuitively, of how to resolve a difficult situation. It is simply a matter of understanding these relationships in a way that takes into consideration the ties from the past, from past-life associations.

"In a similar way as we were speaking (earlier) about another student and his relationship with his girlfriend and her mother, now we have another situation where the mother—yourself—has the relationship with the daughter, and is concerned and wants to see the daughter grow up in a positive and healthy way. You are concerned that this may not happen in the situation that is presently taking place. But you have to realize that your daughter, although seemingly still a child to you, is actually a very old soul. A child may only be several years old in their present body and yet their psychic body is made up of countless billions of experiences from possibly thousands of lifetimes. They have the prerogative to gain the lessons of life for themselves in the way that they need to learn them.

"Not that you should be heartless and throw your child out onto the street, and say sink or swim! It is important to learn how to take your own desires to shape and mold this small person, and let go of the restrictions that are a misconception on your part as to the needs of your daughter.

"We can say that in a past lifetime, you had a situation in which you had gotten involved with an individual who was one of the mercenaries who were traveling around Europe in the 1400s, when sword play was very popular. He would give his abilities to the highest bidder, and you became involved with this individual, as you were impressed with the flamboyant way that he lived his life. You did have a child together. As this child grew, you began to lose respect in your relationship to this person, and you saw that he was very much involved in activities that were of a very violent nature. This was not a good environment for a child to grow up in, and he was not willing to change.

"You became very concerned about your daughter and raised these problems with the father, and he did not accept your concerns as having any importance. Eventually he left and took the daughter with him on a quest to another country and he gave his allegiance to a king of that distant land.

"Your daughter was taken from you, so now you are overly concerned with the association with the subtle psychic memory of this past. You have developed a positive polarity with this daughter, as you have known each other in previous lives, and you have been helpful to each other. In this past, you experienced a great loss because you never saw your daughter again. Your husband settled in another country and you never received any word from them as to where you could find your daughter.

"Does this information help at all in giving you some insight as to why you feel so concerned about your daughter? Do you have any other questions relative to this information?"

(Leslie has a tearful releasement and relates that this has been her great fear, that she would lose her daughter again.)

Leslie: "Thank you very much; this helps a lot."

Brothers: "We would like to relate that tears are the universal catalyst for spiritual healing, as the body is made up of approximately seventy percent water. Emotional releasement through crying is helping to clear away and rectify these aberrant wave forms in the psychic body. The psychic is being cleansed and purified and you should feel free of this particular problem.

"Well, I believe the time is running out for this evening's session. We would again reiterate that you should allow yourself to feel the great healing, Love radiations of the Universal Brotherhood. Try to realize that this Love is simply a thought away, just a simple thought away are these angelic teachers, who only want your own best progress. They are looking out for you in all ways.

"It is the purpose of each person to learn to develop and establish this attunement with

A wise man knows what he doesn't know.

—Benjamin Franklin

these principles of energy as it oscillates from the positive to the negative pole, and to learn to rectify the aberrations which cause all diseased conditions, both mental and physical. This is a long-term project—and please have patience with yourself! It will take time to reacquaint yourself with these teachings which you have known and used in previous lives.

"We would like to express our appreciation for your dedication toward your own overcoming of your past, and we wish you the most positive radiations of Light, that they will be with you and lead you continuously forward on your own spiritual path. Thank you."

—The Universal Brotherhood of Light

THE EYE OF THE INFINITE

The Celestial Teaching Centers

The spiritual worlds have been known as heaven, the summerland, the happy hunting grounds, Valhalla, and countless other names related to different religions and belief systems of various cultures.

The Celestial Teaching Centers exist on countless planets and are huge educational centers where we can learn about our progressive spiritual development. As our spirit leaves our body in "death," we evolve into the spiritual dimensions that are compatible with our level of understanding. It matters little what name we call it, as the importance is in our sincere desire to let go of dogmatic and rhetorical thought patterns. With this dedication to self-improvement we can expand our perspective with new concepts, refining our psychic body into higher and more ethereal vibrations or frequencies, which are compatible with even more advanced dimensions and worlds.

CELESTIAL TEACHING CENTERS

The Importance of Developing Positive Polarities—Twin Flames or Soulmates

The terms "soulmate" or "twin flame" can also be understood in the more scientific format of "polarity," or "biocentric polarity." What this refers to is the affinity that the soul develops with another individual throughout many hundreds or thousands of lifetimes as they reincarnate together as husband and wife, father and daughter, or any other family relationships. Your soulmate can even be your best friend.

Although you can and usually do develop a polarity with many different people, it is based on positive and negative experiences that you have shared together, both in the physical and spiritual worlds. It is usually the reason for feeling an immediate attraction to another person or a strong sense of familiarity,

but past associations also carry the negative repercussions of emotional trauma, i.e. abandonment, betrayal, cruelty, even murder. This is why a relationship that begins on a positive, loving note oftentimes turns sour and leads to a breakup.

In a true positive relationship or polarity with another person, it is similar to a battery or magnet where two opposite poles together form a powerful union. In the case of soulmates, or positive polarities, their unified efforts build up a tremendous charge of energy that they both can draw from to help them carry out important creative or spiritual work. In a sense, they help balance each other as they move into higher and more creative states of consciousness.

TWIN SOULS

On Channeling

I have striven not to laugh at human actions, not to weep at them, nor to hate them, but to understand them.

—Baruch Spinoza

The actual mechanics behind the process of becoming a clear channel is something that would be very beneficial to understand and to learn about. Because everybody is a channel, everyone is relating information from a circuit that can be called the memory consciousness, and that memory consciousness is functioning on a specific frequency. As you are going through your daily life and communicating to your fellow humans, you are channeling information from your own subconscious, which is your memory consciousness.

Now to take this understanding a little farther would be to become aware that there is an infinite spark of intelligence that is the developmental spiritual self of each individual. This is the Superconsciousness, which is a development over many thousands of lifetimes; it is the positive, developed, learning experiences that each soul has accumulated and established as a unified field of knowledge. In other words, it has become a positive association of waveforms within their psychic bodies. These positively-biased waveforms are in tune and harmonically related with the Infinite Creative Intelligence, and which has been known as God in your past civilizations.

It is actually a natural process to begin to attune your mind to the higher spiritual frequencies as they are constantly being radiated from those Angelic minds living in the higher-dimensional worlds. This higher mental attunement is something that everyone should be striving to make, in whatever way they can.

Everyone has their own methods and means that they have set up, before they incarnated into their present physical bodies, to be some type of channel, whether it is in art, writing, teaching, etc. It might be just simply speaking to others about the spiritual principles that you are learning. Fear, along with any of the lower emotions, when allowed access to your mind, will short-circuit the connection to the higher, sublime thoughts that automatically attune you to your positive higher self. Fear is that insidious emotion that, when allowed to be established in your thoughts for any period of time, has a magnetic attraction to other individuals who are also fearful. This is how the syndrome known as paranoia is established; it is an association with other people who have died, now on the spirit side, living without physical bodies, and yet they have that same frequency of fear that attracts them to any similar, negative frequency.

Just as a bee is attracted to pollen in its innate expression of nature, so is the fearful entity attracted to its natural affiliation with other, like-minded souls. Obviously, this fear syndrome is a regressive form of expression and it is only through facing and overcoming these fears that true spiritual progress is made.

Therefore, "channeling" can be understood as a simple process and one that will be extremely beneficial when you can integrate these concepts as a working principle into your life. Because as you think, so you are; in other words, you are building your future by the thoughts you express today.

Everyone has an infinite spiritual spark that is their higher self. That spark is the everlasting, eternal essence of life which can eventually grow into a great illumined flame of Love in the future eons of time, as you devote yourself to your own progressive evolution.

COMMUNION

The belief in Angels has experienced a tremendous resurgence in our present day as we race into the 21st century. Diverse opinions arise as to just what Angels are and where they come from—although most agree they are ever at work, inspiring, uplifting, and uniquely expressing their loving guidance into our too often-troubled existence.

Some see Angels as fairy-like beings living a paradisiacal lifestyle, being specially ordained by God—their only purpose being flying between heaven and earth, helping humankind in countless miraculous ways to remain steadfast in their mission of spiritual liberation.

Others see Angels as evolved humans who, through countless eons of time, have perfected their awareness of the scientific principles of life, harmonizing their minds in a totally positive, progressive unity with nature and the universe. They do not necessarily have the familiar form of human beings but can appear in various ethereal shapes, from brilliant, pulsating globes of light to tiny, golden specks that dance around your hands as you read some particularly inspiring book. Or an intense, blinding galaxy of pure radiant light that boggles the mind of the viewer as they receive telepathic messages and visions of the past, present, or future. It can generally be surmised that the recipient of these visions will receive information compatible with their own knowledge and beliefs.

However they may appear to us, most can agree that Angels work tirelessly, maintaining the vast complex cosmos, helping others in lower states of awareness to awaken to their true spiritual nature. Theirs is not a life of indolence and ease but a never-ending exploration of the knowledge necessary for attaining self-mastery. Starting out in their embryonic beginnings as a human being, they can, after millions of years of spiritual, evolutionary progression, become those great illumined beings creating universes in the exalted nature of their thoughts—thus helping millions in the lower levels of existence to strive for similar attainments and to eventually become Angels themselves.

TEMPLE OF THE ETERNAL GOLDEN FLAMES

CELESTIAL WORLDS

The scientist doesn't study nature because it is useful. He studies it because he delights in it, and he delights in it because it is beautiful.
—Henri Poincare

ARCHANGEL'S LOVELIGHT

Angels, Guides, and Masters

(The following was channeled through the author-artist from the Universal Brotherhood.)

Brothers: "On a beam of Light we greet you, and in a momentary flash of so-called microseconds we are here with you! As usual in these contacts, we are interested in establishing a learning process so that each individual who is listening to or reading these words, through their own desire to progress themselves on the spiritual path, will have that opportunity.

"We come to you as a coterie of Spiritual Brothers and Sisters, and in this unified consciousness we speak together as one, although we are many. We no longer function under the limitations of an earth body or an earth consciousness.

"You have been searching for many lifetimes for this curriculum, as it has not been available in its present scientific form for many thousands of years! These teachings were known of and taught in the school systems during the civilization of Atlantis more than fifteen thousand years ago, and we could go back even much further than this. It is strictly through the great mastership of Archangel Raphiel, also known as Jesus of Nazareth, and Archangel Uriel, that these teachings have found their way into your earth planet.

"These two, Raphiel and Uriel, along with Archangels Michiel and Muriel, are the Hierarchical God forces from the supercelestial worlds who have projected the healing balm of Love to anyone and everyone who has dedicated themselves to their own progressive, spiritual development.

"All four of these Advanced Intellects incarnated into physical bodies in your twentieth century as a means of setting in motion the New Age for humankind. They have all now released themselves from the strictures of these physical bodies and have ascended into their proper positions in the higher spiritual worlds. Be not concerned that they have removed their physical bodies from your sight, but rest assured that you can contact them from your inner sight, and this will always be the case, beyond all space and time.

"You may not have met these great Brothers in their more recent incarnations and yet you can feel the Spirit of their consciousness, as it has been literally impinged into the very fabric of the electromagnetic spectrum of your earth planet. This is an ultra-high frequency to which you can attune in all your positive spiritual efforts, and this great Love vibration will transform everything and everyone it touches, enlightening them with a new hope and faith in their positive future.

"This is not a personality that we are speaking of but an infinite consciousness which is a great transmitting source of Love and Light to all who have learned the methods of tuning in to this power which has been known as 'God.'

"These great God Forces could be described as functioning from the eleventh level or dimension of mastership, and as you are familiar with the third dimension, which is your present position, it would be impossible for you to conceive of the great splendor in which these Angelic forces live!

"The brilliance of the Light that these Masters are constantly radiating is a Light that can guide you, and it will guide you, but the difficulty is in perceiving this Light. We are speaking of worlds where there is no night, and in this eternally lighted atmosphere, our minds are positively attuned to the Fountainhead as we look ahead to our own future expansion and spiritual progression—never ending!

OVERSHADOWING HEALING PRESENCE

The wisest man in the world is the man who knows himself.
                    —Socrates

"We realize these expanded states of consciousness are beyond your present conception but we also were once like you and had to make the incremental evolutionary progress that you now are making. The consciousness of URIEL is a Universal Radiant Infinite Eternal Light. She has had a leading role in the spiritualization of your planet Earth, as she has spent hundreds of lifetimes incarnating in physical bodies to accomplish this mission. Uriel is a spiritual force that is so integrated with this Infinite Creative Intelligence that we have been attempting to describe, that she is literally helping to sustain and energize the cosmos as it exists infinitely as planets, stars, galaxies, universes, and people!

"The purpose of these dissertations is to stimulate your minds in the process of learning and expanding the more primitive concepts that have been the basic structures of your past-life histories. This learning process can be developed very easily by simply opening your mind to new possibilities and not being distracted by the many illusions that the material world creates when you fail to recognize the spiritual energy system that is the true you. This is difficult to realize when you are enamored by the physical consciousness, as the past holds many blocks that must be eventually recognized and overcome. This is how spiritual progress is made.

"Your reality is relative to the security you feel, which is based upon the many past lives lived, oblivious to your true spiritual nature. Reality is not a concrete concept, as most people believe. Reality is actually fluid when your mind is functioning from your higher self, constantly changing and growing, aligned with nature's constant motion.

"Please realize that it will take time to create a new consciousness and this is what you are constantly doing, as your thoughts and actions of today are building your future. This is why it is so important to learn to attune to your higher creative nature, as this is the means of expanding your mind and harmonizing with those Minds who are functioning as a unified force for good. Build your consciousness well and build it out of the pure substance of spirit, which will constantly rejuvenate your life, renewing your understanding of your true purpose. That purpose is to become enlightened by your efforts in living true to the mission that you set up for yourself in the spiritual worlds before incarnating in your present physical body.

"Love is the pure, spiritual essence from which you can fabricate the necessary pathway which will lead you out of the brambles of the past and into the lighted worlds of your future. We, your Brothers in Spirit, will meet you there with our hands outstretched, welcoming you home!

"May the light of the Infinite always guide your footsteps, leading you onto that never-ending pathway into the stars."
                    —The Universal Brotherhood of Light

Our love of what is beautiful does not lead to extravagance; our love of the things of the mind does not make us soft.

    —Pericles

SPIRIT FALLS

GATHERING AT ANGEL'S COVE

If we find the answer to that (why is it that we and the universe exist?), it would be the ultimate triumph of human reason—for then we would know the mind of God.
—Stephen Hawking

ANGEL'S CALLING

I doubt that there is any word in our vocabulary that causes a more fearful reaction than death. And yet it is as normal and natural as the experience of birth. In fact, the two are inherently tied together; you could never have one without the other. So why are we so terrified of death?

I believe it begins with a general trait of human nature in which the fear of the unknown is reinforced into us from the formative years of our youth. It comes down to a basic ignorance in which our society lacks the knowledge necessary to understand and educate our children about this most natural, and yes, beautiful experience we call "death."

I can speak from my own experience, as my mother died when I was ten years old and I feel certain this event had a greater negative impact on my life than any other experience. We didn't talk about it or treat it as a natural part of life, but went into denial and acted as if our mother never existed. We never again talked about her or this terrible event. I was left with severe nightmares after my mother's death that affected me in a much greater way than I understood at the time. It was only after I became much more dedicated to my spiritual growth that this incident began to be slowly brought back into my consciousness and the healing process could begin.

In beginning to realize and understand that we are eternal, spiritual beings that evolve through countless lifetimes, many of the pieces of the puzzle of my life began to fall into place. Since my youth, I had been having dreams that proved to me that I existed beyond the confines of my physical body. I had on several occasions seen my body lying on the bed as I floated up to the ceiling of my room in what is commonly called astral projection.

One experience that left a powerful impact on my life was when a good friend of mine who had died appeared to me in a dream. It was quite an amazing experience, as in the dream I saw a window begin to open up and my deceased friend appeared and told me to come with him as he had some things to show me. He looked radiant, with a beautiful smile, and I asked him how he could be with me when he had died several years before. He took me by the hand and began showing me around the world in which he now lived. He explained that death was simply a transition from one state of consciousness to another. It was not something to be feared but a natural part of life in the earth worlds. He now lived in what is commonly called the astral worlds, and he said he was much happier now than he had ever been in his earth-life existence.

I marveled at the beautiful, joyous atmosphere and the radiant sparkle that seemed to be reflected from all the objects in this world, especially the people! He took me to his house and I met his girlfriend and other members of his spiritual family. It was obvious that life on the other side was very similar to our side of existence. As I awoke from this fascinating dream, I knew that I had just experienced life after death and my friend was not "dead" but was carrying on his life as the eternal, spiritual being that he and all of us truly are. Death is just another unique episode in the ongoing great adventure of life.

A friend asked me to do a portrait of her deceased brother, Jose. As I worked on the painting, I felt Jose's presence and the beautiful soul he is. He was an artist, and the way the painting came through was interesting as it portrayed his past-life associations in the Mayan culture, symbolized in the Mayan Temple Pyramid in the upper right side of the painting. In his hand, he holds a paint brush with which he creates a beautiful rainbow across the desert sky in his home state of Arizona.

SPIRIT PORTRAIT OF JOSE

There is no worse lie than a truth
misunderstood by those who hear it.
—William James

The artist at work

I have had the opportunity to do several large murals and have found working large to be extremely stimulating and rewarding. Sometimes the inspiration flows so rapidly the painting seems to have a mind of its own and is completed in a very short period of time. I simply consider myself a humble channel for the inspiration that can flow through me, or anyone who learns the principles involved in becoming a channel for the Light.

About the Artist

Douglas Taylor was born in Long Beach, California, in 1953. He grew up with a deep love for the ocean and a fascination for metaphysical subjects. In his late teens, he began work as a carpenter and this seasonal trade allowed him the freedom to travel the world for the next ten years enjoying his favorite pastime, surfing. His travels stimulated his adventurous spirit and he developed a profound appreciation for nature and its healing and rejuvenating effects in his life. He also began having many strange and wonderful psychic experiences that opened the door to the next step in his spiritual progression.

At age thirty, with no previous creative or artistic background, Douglas began his first attempts at writing and painting. His creative channel opened up and his painting and writing improved very rapidly. He sold fourteen paintings at his first art showing!

Now some fourteen years later, he teaches classes, gives workshops and does slide-show lectures as a way of connecting with other, like-minded souls. These expressions have been received most positively and considered spiritually empowering by those who attend. Douglas feels very fortunate in being able to develop his artistic abilities and simply considers himself a channel for the spiritual agencies that work with anyone who is sincere in their efforts to improve themselves.

"Art has the power to transform the mundane daily existence into a wonderland of creative possibilities where the mind soars free, unfettered by limitations," says Douglas.

Please send your questions and comments to:
Douglas Taylor
1846 Main Street,
Huntington Beach, CA 92648
Or E-mail: dougt@surfside.net

PEGASUS

On wings of light we sail
Flying free beyond the Earth's travail
The starlight guides our flight
Courageously we move into the night
We are the masters of our own fate
Our inner strength will open freedom's gate
Now our path is clear within our sight
As in truth we merge with the eternal light